THE NATIONAL TRUST
BOOK OF
The
ARMADA

MARY CONNATTY

Illustrated by
Richard Hook,
Richard Scollins,
Tony Bryant and
Malcolm Porter

KINGFISHER BOOKS

Contents

First published in 1987 by Kingfisher Books Limited, Elsley House, 24–30 Great Titchfield Street, London W1P 7AD, a Grisewood and Dempsey Company, in association with The National Trust for Places of Historic Interest or Natural Beauty, 36 Queen Anne's Gate, London SW1H 9AS.

© Grisewood and Dempsey Limited 1987

BRITISH LIBRARY CATALOGUING IN PUBLICATION DATA
Connatty, Mary
    The National Trust Book of the Armada.
    1. Armada, 1588 – Juvenile literature
    I. Title II. National Trust
    942.05'5   DA360
    ISBN 0-86272-282-9

Edited by Deborah Manley
Designed by Ben White
Printed in Italy by Vallardi Industrie Grafiche, Milan

The publishers wish to thank the following for supplying photographs for this book: 3 National Portrait Gallery London; by kind permission of the Marquess of Tavistock and the Trustees of the Bedford Estates; 6 reproduced by Gracious Permission of Her Majesty the Queen; 7 British Library; 8 top National Portrait Gallery, London; bottom National Maritime Museum, London; 11 Michael Holford; 13 top Bibliotèque Nationale, Paris, bottom Rijkürchief in Zuid-Holland; 14 top National Portrait Gallery, London, bottom Collection: Plymouth City Museum and Art Gallery; 15 National Maritime Museum, London; 17 MAS, Barcelona; 18 English Heritage; 19 British Library; 20 The Huntington Library, San Marino, California; 25 Courtesy of the Marquess of Salisbury; 28 left National Maritime Museum, London, right British Library; 29 and 32 National Maritime Museum, London; 35 National Trust; 36 Ulster Museum, Belfast; 38 by kind permission of the Marquess of Tavistock and the Trustees of the Bedford Estates; 39 National Portrait Gallery, London.

Author's Note

All dates given in this book are according to the Gregorian or New Style Calendar, announced by Pope Gregory XIII in 1582. Almost all Europe was using the Gregorian Calendar by 1587.

England continued to use the Old Style (Julian) Calendar until 1751, so until this date English documents are according to the Old Style.

The Old Style (Julian) Calendar, devised by Julius Caesar in 46 BC, took as the length of the lunar year 365 days, 5 hours, 48 minutes and 46 seconds.

By the sixteenth century the discrepancy amounted to ten days, so, for us today, the English usage of the Julian Calendar gives an incorrect reading of time and weather.

I have chosen the New Style or Gregorian because we use it today and because it corresponds with the actual time and weather conditions of the voyage and battles of the Armada.

Introduction

In the summer of 1588, King Philip II of Spain sent the Great Armada, or armed fleet, to conquer England. This book tells the story of that "great enterprise". It describes the events which led up to the despatch of the Armada, beginning with the developing conflict between England and Spain over the previous century. The story unfolds as the European sea powers battled for world supremacy in religion, trade and territory.

Philip II had several reasons for grievance where England was concerned. Religion was of prime importance. Sixteenth century Europe was torn apart by the split between Catholics and Protestants. Henry VIII rejected the power of the Pope and made himself head of the Church in England. Spain remained Catholic and the fanatically religious Philip wanted to make England return to the old faith.

The second important reason was competition for supremacy in trade and sea power. Spain's discovery of the New World opened up a huge source of trade, of which the English wanted a share. The growing expertise of English naval power was a threat to Spain's domination of the seas. Of crucial importance was England's strategic position. With England in his grasp, Philip could command the Channel, encircle Spain's old enemy, France, and have easy passage to the Spanish Netherlands.

Philip's decision to send the Armada was not taken lightly. It was an incredible undertaking. We see how plans went wrong, and how ships were at the mercy of the weather.

There is no doubt that, had the Armada succeeded, Philip would have got rid of Queen Elizabeth. As it turned out its failure was to be to Elizabeth's advantage, and she cleverly turned it into a great English victory. When she died England was established as a great and growing power. For Spain the tide had turned. Though still dominant in Europe, the disaster of the "Invincible" Armada marked the beginning of her decline.

Philip II of Spain
and Elizabeth I
of England

1: The Contenders

Dynasties

One hundred years before the Great Armada sailed to England, Henry VII, the first Tudor king, wanted to expand his power through an alliance with Spain. Ferdinand and Isabella of Spain wanted Henry as an ally against France. So they arranged a marriage for their daughter, Catherine of Aragon, with the heir to the English throne, Arthur, Prince of Wales.

In 1501 Arthur, then fourteen, and Catherine, who was two years older, were married. Within six months Arthur died. His younger brother, Henry, was now heir to the throne. In 1509, when he was just eighteen, he became king, as Henry VIII, and married his brother's widow, Catherine. They wanted a son to keep the Tudor dynasty strong and lasting, but sadly only one of their children, Mary, survived.

Then Henry wanted to put aside Catherine and marry again. When the Pope refused to annul his marriage, Henry made himself head of the church, divorced Catherine and married Anne Boleyn, hoping for a son. The Pope and Catholic leaders declared his marriage to Anne illegal, and their daughter, Elizabeth,

The Tudor family symbol was the rose. Henry VII of Lancaster ended the Wars of the Roses by marrying Elizabeth of York. The red rose of Lancaster was linked with the white rose of York to form the Tudor rose.

The lions and castles of Castile were the important symbols of Spain. Catherine of Aragon's personal sign was the pomegranate, symbol of fertility.

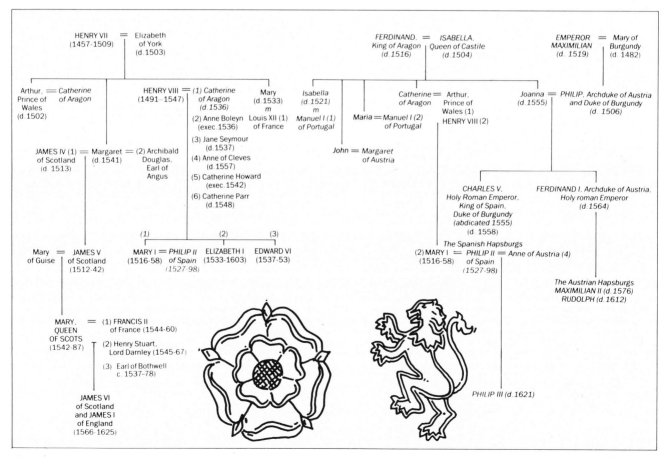

4

On July 15, 1554 Phillip II of Spain and Mary I of England were married in Winchester Cathedral. Royal marriages were arranged, normally by the parents, for reasons of politics, religion and economics. It was unusual that Mary arranged her own marriage with her cousin, but she was already a queen and 37 years old. Philip was nine years younger and a widower. Both were devout Catholics and wanted to make England Catholic again, but Mary very foolishly did not consult many of her advisers, not realizing that Philip's reasons for wanting the marriage were coldly political, but much to his annoyance, Parliament refused to have him crowned King of England.

illegitimate, with no right to the throne. Henry's divorce from Catherine and his declaration that their daughter, Mary, was a bastard with no right to succeed him, were deep insults to Spain.

In 1536 Henry had Anne Boleyn beheaded for adultery and married his third wife, Jane Seymour. Their son, Edward, became king when Henry died in 1547. During Edward's reign England was strongly Protestant, but he died in 1553 when he was only fifteen and his older half-sister became Queen Mary I.

Mary, the child of Catherine of Aragon, had strong support from Spain. Being half-Spanish, she wanted their friendship and in 1554, she married her cousin, Philip of Spain. His father, Charles V, had counselled him to marry Mary and renew the English–Spanish alliance as a counterbalance against France. Both Philip and Mary thought it their duty to bring England back to Catholicism.

The marriage was unpopular in England because the people hated the Spanish influence. Philip visited England only twice. He was never crowned King of England and did not have

power to change English law. However, he involved England with a war with France, in which England lost Calais. This was an immense blow to national prestige, and Mary was blamed. She believed her troubles were God's punishment for the Protestant heresy of her people and increased her drive against Protestants. She had over 300 people burned at the stake for their religious beliefs, earning herself the name "Bloody Mary".

When Mary died in 1558 her Protestant half-sister, Elizabeth, became queen. Philip II, anxious to maintain the alliance, suggested marriage to her. She refused, disliking his strong Catholicism and determined to keep England independent. Tensions increased between England and Spain. The Pope excommunicated Elizabeth in 1570, and she responded by making laws against the Catholics. English Catholics who fled abroad turned to Spain for help to bring the faith back to England. They wanted the Catholic Mary Queen of Scots to be Queen of England. Spain, eager to influence politics and religion in England, supported Mary's claim to the throne.

Elizabeth and Mary Queen of Scots

Before Henry VIII died he made a will stating the succession in the following order: Edward, Mary, and Elizabeth. Most Catholics regarded Elizabeth as illegitimate with no right to succeed. When Mary died in 1558, Elizabeth became queen and her right was challenged by Catholics who supported Mary Queen of Scots, who had a claim to the English throne because her grandmother was Henry VIII's sister.

Mary became Queen of the Scots in 1542 when she was a tiny baby. When she was six she was taken to France for her safety. She was brought up a Catholic and treated as a queen in the grand manner of the French court. At sixteen she married the heir to the French throne, who became Francis II a year later. The following year Francis died and, at seventeen, Mary was a widow. She returned to Scotland in 1561, and her presence there was a great threat to Elizabeth.

While Mary was in France, her mother, the French Mary of Guise, ruled in her place. This gave France immense power over affairs in Scotland, which was resented by many Scottish nobles. A great number of them supported the new Protestant religion. Mary at first took a moderate line with the different religious groups, as Elizabeth was trying to do in England, but English Catholics were commanded by the Pope not to recognize Elizabeth as their queen. She responded by outlawing the practice

Mary, Queen of Scots was moved from one prison to another in England. Her jailor was the Earl of Shrewsbury, whose wife, the celebrated Bess of Hardwick, spent many hours sewing with Mary. Their embroidery can be seen at Hardwick Hall, Derbyshire and Oxburgh Hall, Norfolk.

of the Catholic faith. Many English Catholics who wished to have Elizabeth as their queen were put in a very difficult position.

In Scotland, Mary married her cousin, Lord Darnley, who also had a claim to the English throne. To begin with this marriage was supported by Catholics. They had one son, James. His birth strengthened her position, but Darnley was weak and ambitious, and they quarrelled bitterly. When Darnley was murdered in 1567, it was thought that Mary was involved in the plot. People became more suspicious when she married the Earl of Bothwell, who was certainly involved in Darnley's murder. Mary was forced off the throne, and her infant son became James VI of Scotland. Mary fled south, hoping Elizabeth would help her regain the Scottish throne. It was a wild dream.

Mary became one of Elizabeth's greatest problems. If she allowed Mary to go free, Catholics would have access to her and the opportunity to dethrone Elizabeth. Mary was imprisoned and, for eighteen years while Elizabeth's followers wanted to get rid of her, Catholics plotted against Elizabeth.

The Pope, Philip II of Spain and English Catholics in exile were all involved in efforts to free Mary to establish her as Queen of Scotland and make her Queen of England. Most of these plots were made abroad and came to nothing. In 1586 a more serious affair occurred. Anthony Babington, a young gentleman from Derbyshire, conspired to free Mary, to "despatch the usurping Competitor" (Elizabeth) and put Mary on the throne. The plot was discovered; Babington and his friends were condemned to be hanged, drawn and quartered. Mary was tried and executed.

Mary's execution shocked Europe. Catholics looked upon her as a martyr. Philip II felt obliged to avenge her death. At the same time, Mary's death left him free to claim the English throne.

Elizabeth was very reluctant to have Mary, Queen of Scots put to death. Mary was her cousin and of royal blood. But Mary's presence in England was a great stumbling block to peace. Many powerful Catholics supported her, but Protestant nobles wanted her out of the way. Their opportunity came with the discovery of the Babington Plot. Mary was involved and tried for treason and found guilty. Elizabeth delayed signing the death warrant, but she did so at last on January 22, 1587. The sentence was carried out quickly and Mary went to her execution with great courage. Here she is being brought to her execution and prepared for her beheading. In contrast to the wretchedness of her imprisonment, Mary was given a grand state funeral at Peterborough Cathedral. In 1612 her son, James I, had her coffin removed to Westminster Abbey where it lies beneath a sumptuous white marble monument.

The Growth of Power in Tudor England

Henry VII, the first Tudor monarch, was determined to expand his riches and power by increasing trade. England was then an agricultural country with a population of about 3,000,000. English merchants grew rich from the export of woollen cloth, and the King filled his treasury from the customs duty charged on the exports. The Merchant Adventurers of London dominated the wool trade, and Antwerp in the Netherlands was the great port through which English merchandise entered Europe.

A shortage of English ships forced merchants to ship their goods in foreign vessels, such as those of the Hanseatic League, which had depots in England and in the ports of northern Europe. Henry VII introduced Navigation Acts in 1485 and 1489 to encourage English merchants to build their own ships to carry their own merchandise. He also took steps to extend trade in Europe by making agreements with France, Portugal and Spain.

Competition was fierce between trading states. When the English began to buy wine, dried fruit and spices from Crete and Middle Eastern countries, they came up against the merchants of Venice, who monopolized trade in the Mediterranean. Henry retaliated by making a treaty with Florence, using the port of Pisa as a depot for English wool.

In 1496 Henry sent John Cabot to explore the east coast of North America, and his discoveries led to the formation of a Bristol company, the Adventurers of the New Found Lands, to extend English trade across the Atlantic.

In Henry VIII's reign the wool trade continued to flourish, but he was more intent on territorial gain than his father. England still

Henry VIII spent lavishly on entertainments and pageants. He loved music and feasting and employed many artists to decorate his great palaces. As a young man he was tall and splendidly athletic, with golden hair and glowing skin. He lived too well and his huge suit of armour in the Tower of London shows his enormous size in old age.

The proudest ship of Henry VIII's navy was the *Henry Grace à Dieu*, nicknamed *Great Harry*. It was launched at Woolwich in 1514, a huge, high-built, ship, weighing 1500 tons and carrying 184 guns and a crew of 700. Later, in the time of Henry's daughter, Elizabeth I, warships became lower, leaner and swifter.

owned Calais and a piece of surrounding territory, and Henry was eager to extend his power into France. He made two attempts to regain French territory and had great battleships like the *Henri Grace à Dieu* and the *Mary Rose* built for that purpose. He also had a series of forts, blockhouses and castles erected along the south coast. These were later reinforced by Elizabeth as defence against the Spaniards.

When Mary I was queen she lost Calais to the French, but exploration for trade routes was renewed. In 1554 Richard Chancellor sailed north-east to Archangel to open up trade with Russia. He visited Moscow and was received at the court of Ivan the Terrible.

After Mary died and Elizabeth became queen, England entered the competition for world markets. Elizabeth employed the experienced John Hawkins to build up her navy. At that time there was little difference between merchant and fighting ships, because merchant vessels carried arms for defence against pirates, and in times of war they could easily be converted into battleships. English ships were designed to be faster than the Spanish, and, though England and Spain were officially at peace, English ships attacked Spanish treasure ships returning from the New World. This further increased the growing tension between the two countries.

One of the toughest competitors to the English was the Hanseatic League, a group of German merchants who dominated the Baltic and north European trade. The Hanseatic League had bases like this one in London, Southampton and Boston in Lincolnshire.

2: Background to History

The Age of Discovery

The sixteenth century was a period of great expansion for Europe. The known world, which had until then been only Europe, Asia and Africa, was opened up by the new great voyages of discovery.

In 1452 Ferdinand and Isabella of Spain sent Christopher Columbus in command of three small ships to find a western route to Asia. After two months at sea Columbus sighted land and thought he had reached the eastern coast of Asia. He was wrong.

He had discovered islands of a new world unknown to Europeans. The first island which Columbus came to was probably San Salvador in the Bahamas. Weeks later he reached Cuba and Haiti. He called these islands the West Indies. On his three further voyages he discovered more islands and the mainland of South America and Central America. Until his death he believed that these lands previously unknown to Europe were a part of Asia. Soon other adventurers were following excitedly in the footsteps of Columbus or seeking other new lands.

In 1497 Vasco da Gama, a Portuguese, rounded the Cape of Good Hope and sailed up the coast of East Africa and across the Indian Ocean to Goa on the coast of India.

The Spanish continued to look for a route to Asia across the Atlantic and eventually, in 1520, Ferdinand Magellan found the route by sailing around the tip of South America, through the strait which was to be named after him, and then out into the

The map shows the routes of the great explorers and the territory colonized or dominated by Spain and Portugal in the sixteenth century. Portugal was more interested in trade than settlement. For Spain, with her huge population, America was an outlet for adventurous men and women, eager to get rich. Both countries wanted riches, but the conversion of the heathen to Christianity was equally important. But often human greed was stronger than the desire to convert the pagans who were reduced to slavery.

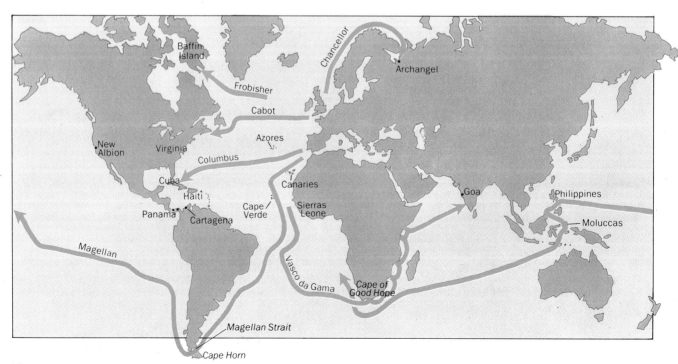

This early map of South America and the Strait of Magellan shows how little was known of the geography of the New World. Imaginary animals inhabit the land, and on the tree hangs the coat-of-arms of Spain.

In 1519, Ferdinand Magellan, a Portuguese paid by the Spanish, set sail westwards to find a passage to the Spice Islands. He found a way round the tip of South America through the Strait now named after him. It is 350 miles long with high cliffs making a wind tunnel that creates appalling storms. In 1521 when Magellan sailed out of the Strait into calm water he named the new sea the Pacific (or peaceful) ocean. He was killed later in the Phillipines, but his fleet reached Spain the following year, to complete the first round the world voyage.

When the Spanish first discovered Central and South America they made friends with the natives, but when they needed labour for their plantations and mines, they forced the natives to work. As more labourers were needed, slaves were brought by traders from the west of Africa. Before the trade was stopped in the nineteenth century, over 10,000,000 slaves had been taken to the Americas.

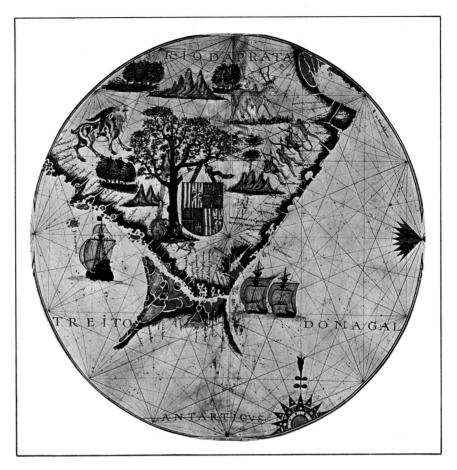

Pacific Ocean. Magellan was killed in the Philippines, but one of his ships reached Spain in 1522, having completed the first round the world voyage.

In 1576 Martin Frobisher, a tough Yorkshireman, reached Baffin Island, and one year later Francis Drake set out on the three-year journey which made him the first Englishman to circumnavigate the world.

When the Spanish discovered gold and silver in Mexico and Peru other European seafaring nations were eager to take part in the trade, but Spain, first on the scene in the New World, was unwilling to share her wealth.

World trade was now taking over from European trade, but for the English the slave trade off the coast of West Africa was a profitable source of wealth. The Spanish settlers in the West Indies and South America needed labour badly on their plantations and in the silver mines, and John Hawkins and others provided this "merchandise".

After 1580, when Philip II annexed Portugal, Spanish territories in the New World stretched from the basin of the Mississippi River in North America down to the mouth of the Rio de la Plata in Argentina. Spain became the undisputed Catholic power in the world, to whom the Pope looked for religious zeal and political support.

Spain and her Allies

Ferdinand and Isabella of Spain had greatly expanded their power, through marriage alliances and by expansion into the New World. Their grandson, Emperor Charles V, split these vast territories between his brother and his son Philip. In 1556 Philip became King Philip II of Spain, the Spanish Netherlands and King of the Two Sicilies. With the land owned by Spain in the Americas, he ruled the largest kingdom in Christendom.

His marriage to Mary Tudor was intended to extend Spanish power into England, but Mary's death brought this alliance to an end. Philip wanted to dominate England, but he had wanted to do it peacefully, and he did not, in any case, have enough money to make war at that time.

From 1580 the immense influx of silver into Spain from Peru and Mexico encouraged Philip to expand his power. In 1580 he took Portugal and Spanish troops attacked Smerwick Harbour in Ireland. The English commander slaughtered most of the Spanish garrison after their surrender, and this deepened the tension.

Before Mary Queen of Scots was executed in 1587, she named Philip as her successor to the English throne. This meant that, in the eyes of the Catholic church, he was legal monarch of England. With England in his grasp, Spain would be in a splendid position to send troops to suppress the rebellious Netherlands.

Philip II was an ageing man of sixty when he planned the Great Armada. He carried on his work in a simple study deep inside his grand palace of the Escorial near Madrid. To this lonely room came messengers from his ambassadors in London, Paris and Rome, from Parma in the Netherlands, keeping him informed of English naval strength, of English troops in the Netherlands and of the activities of Catholic exiles in Rome. The information was often misleading and, in the gloomy isolation of his palace, he became gradually out of touch with the world. The failure of the Armada was partly due to Philip's lack of contact with his captains. Had he visited the ports and inspected the progress of preparations he would have been aware of the shortcomings of his plans.

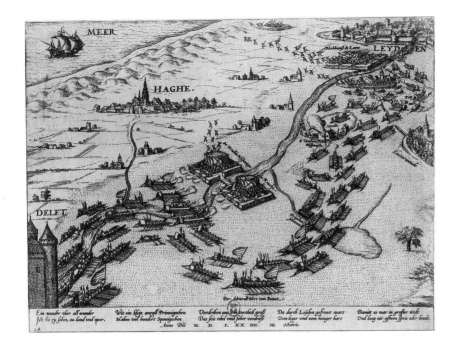

The Sea Beggars were secretly helped by Elizabeth I, who allowed them to shelter in English ports. English volunteers fought alongside the Dutch against the Spanish troops in the Netherlands, and Dutch refugees flocked into England. Justin of Nassau, Admiral of Zeeland, a son of William the Silent, patrolled the shallow waters off the Dutch coast with his flat-bottomed fly boats. Parma's crack troops had little hope of embarking from Neeuport or Dunkirk with Nassau lying in wait.

Troubles in the Spanish Netherlands

The Netherlands was made up of a number of rich and densely populated provinces under Spanish rule. In 1566, the tyrannical rule of Philip II had reached such a pitch that the Dutch people rose in rebellion. Philip, who ruled from faraway Madrid, sent the harsh Duke of Alva to suppress the rebellion and enforce the Catholic faith. This hardened the revolt.

A group of Protestant noblemen, headed by William the Silent, formed a petition to ask for certain rights. They were laughed at as "Beggars" by the Spanish. Furious at such treatment, they formed their own fleet and organized raids on Spanish shipping in the English Channel and North Sea, and proudly called themselves the "Sea Beggars". William the Silent tried to keep the Netherlands united, but the northern states broke away and became Protestant. William was assassinated in 1584, but his son, Maurice, carried on the revolt.

Officially England and Spain were then at peace. Spanish ships used English ports until a huge shipment of silver was confiscated at Southampton by order of Elizabeth. The Duke of Alva was furious and stopped trade with England.

In 1578 Philip sent the Duke of Parma to win back the Protestants in the Netherlands. Parma's successes were cut short by Philip's plans to invade England.

Philip's great scheme was to sail up the English Channel with a huge force and escort Parma's army across to England. Once on English soil, Parma's expert military leadership and experienced soldiers would play a large part in the conquest of England. The success of the Armada depended on this link up with Parma.

William von Lumey, commander of the Sea Beggars, vowed that he would not cut his hair or his nails until they defeated the Spaniards.

The Great English Sea Captains

Elizabeth I was well aware that England's greatness as a world power depended on a strong sea-going force. Such a force would enable the English to establish valuable trading routes, to spread her influence abroad and to defend her shores. Elizabeth therefore greatly prized her sea captains. The most famous and favoured were cousins: Francis Drake and John Hawkins.

After childhood poverty, living with his family near Chatham in Kent in the hull of a ship, Drake was apprenticed to the master of a ship trading with the northern European ports. He came to know every current and sandbank of the English Channel and the North Sea. When the ship's master died, he left his vessel to Drake, who, like many young sailors of his time, sought his fortune in trade with the New World. His first trip there was with his cousin, John Hawkins, who had a thriving trade in slaves from West Africa to the Spanish settlements in the West Indies and Central America. Hawkins and the Spaniards were breaking the law, for Philip II forbade foreign ships to enter Spanish ports abroad, but the Spaniards needed goods, and slaves to work for them. Hawkins also attacked Spanish treasure ships on their way home from the New World. This was open piracy, but Elizabeth turned a blind eye to it, often sharing in the profits.

In 1567 she even lent two ships to Hawkins when he and Drake went on a slaving expedition. When they had sold most of their cargo, the Spanish ambushed them, sinking all but two of their ships and capturing about 400 men. Drake escaped in the *Judith*; Hawkins followed in the tiny *Minion*. Three months later Drake's battered ship, full of starving and dying men, limped into Plymouth Sound. A month later Hawkins arrived, in even worse condition.

Hawkins now gave up his seafaring career and became Comptroller of the Navy. Drake continued to harrass the Spaniards, growing rich on the spoils and supported by the Queen, which deeply offended the Spanish. In 1577 he set sail on the greatest voyage of his career, the circumnavigation of the world. He followed Magellan's route round Cape Horn. Here storms broke up his fleet, but Drake carried on alone in the *Golden Hinde* to capture Spanish treasure ships off the west coast of South America. He then set off across the unknown Pacific, onwards through the Indian Ocean and around the Cape of Good Hope towards home. On 26 September 1580 he sailed his little ship into Plymouth. For this achievement, Queen Elizabeth knighted Drake.

Then in 1586 Drake led a fleet to Cadiz to destroy Spanish ships. This was the famous "singeing of the King's beard". The havoc caused delayed the Armada by six months. The Spaniards had to make new casks and barrels with unseasoned wood, which soured their water and rotted their food on the voyage of the Armada.

The Spaniards called Sir Francis Drake "Il Draco", the Dragon, and many thought he had a magic mirror in his ship's cabin which helped him to find Spanish treasure convoys.

John Hawkins' knowledge of ships and navigation were invaluable to Elizabeth I. As Comptroller of her navy, he built new ships, lower, longer, and easier to sail.

In February 1586 Drake set out from Plymouth with ships supplied by the Queen, the Earl of Leicester, Sir Walter Raleigh and others. His aim was to take revenge in the New World for Philip's capture of English corn ships the previous year, in the port of Bilbao. The English swarmed into Cartagena, the capital of the Spanish South America, and the inhabitants fled. An English captain wrote, "our pikes were longer than theirs, and our bodies better armed; with which advantage our swords and pikes grew too hard for them and they were driven to give place."

Planning the Invincible Armada

In 1580 Philip II annexed Portugal and added the ships from her splendid navy to the Spanish fleet. Silver from the mines in the New World was bringing in immense wealth. Now Philip, with his Lord High Admiral, Santa Cruz, began to plan the invasion of England, but in 1586 Santa Cruz died and the Duke of Medina Sidonia took his place. He was neither a soldier nor a sailor, but was chosen by Philip as one of the greatest noblemen in Spain. Wisely, he took advice from the experienced commanders.

The execution of Mary Queen of Scots, by order of Elizabeth, in 1587 shocked all Catholic nations. Named by Mary Queen of Scots as her successor, Philip was ready now to establish himself as the rightful King of England. He ordered the Duke of Medina to prepare the great fleet to sail up the English Channel to link up with Parma's army from the Netherlands. Together they would invade England.

The organization of the "Great Enterprise" was a colossal task. Philip sent agents to Germany and Italy to buy cannon, armour, gunpowder, shot, swords and all the weapons of war. He chartered vessels from many European nations.

The main task of the Armada would be to transport soldiers to fight in England. Apart from the 22 great Portuguese and Spanish fighting galleons, there were merchant ships converted for battle. Smaller panaches and zabras were used as messenger ships and also for picket or guard duty.

The great unwieldy, lumbering urcas carried siege guns and equipment intended for land battles. They were filled to bursting point with guns, horses, mules and ammunition.

Collecting the stores and equipment for the Great Armada was a prodigious task. Enough food had to be supplied for six months. 11 million pounds of ships biscuit, 600,000 pounds of salt pork, 40,000 gallons of olive oil, 14,000 barrels of wine were but a part of the necessities for a force of over 30,000 men. The great transport urcas were to be filled with 5000 extra pairs of shoes, 11,000 pairs of sandals, as well as equipment to repair ships, and axes, spades and shovels for digging trenches and sieges.

With the fleet went six surgeons and six physicians, 180 priests as spiritual advisers, 19 Justices and 50 administrators, carefully selected to set up government in England, and 146 young gallants who volunteered for the adventure, and took with them 728 servants.

The Armada was divided into ten squadrons, led by the most famous and experienced commanders of the Spanish forces. In charge of the Biscay ships was Don Juan Martinez de Recalde. Don Pedro de Valdes led the Andalusian ships. Don Miguel de Oquendo, nicknamed the "Glory of the Fleet", was the heroic leader of the Guipuzcoan fleet. One of the most dashing commanders was the young Don Alonso de Leyva, whose task was to take over should Medina be killed or disabled.

The oldest commander was Don Juan Martinez de Recalde who was 62 at the time of the Great Armada.

3: Setting Sail

Key points in England's defences were the castles of Sandgate, Walmer, Deal and Dover. Deal Castle, built by Henry VIII in 1539–40, was restored in the 1580s. It is typical of the massive, squat fortifications of Henry's time. Its enormously thick walls and rounded bastions were designed to deflect gunshot (see below). Other work was done in restoring Dover pier, adding a stone quay and gun platform to Portsmouth, and renewing defences on the Isle of Wight, at Southampton, Brownsea Island, Portland, Plymouth and at Pendennis Castle and St Mawes in Cornwall.

The Defence of England

With the renewed threat from Spain in the 1580s, England had begun to step up her defences. The attack was expected from the south, so all along the coast from Cornwall to the mouth of the Thames the castles, forts and blockhouses of Henry VIII's time were restored. The prime target of Philip II's troops must be the capture of London, so its defences were of the utmost importance.

The blockhouses at East Mersea and West Tilbury were repaired and Queenborough Castle on the Isle of Sheppey was reinforced to protect London. The only new fort built in Elizabeth's reign was at Upnor on the Medway, especially designed to guard the new naval dockyard at Chatham.

There was no standing army in England so armed bands or militia were organized locally. The Queen's great favourite, Robert Dudley, Earl of Leicester, was given the important task of defending London and the Queen. Leicester had his main force at Tilbury. He had led a force against the experienced troops of

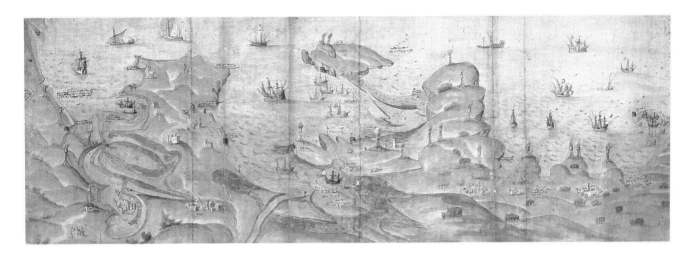

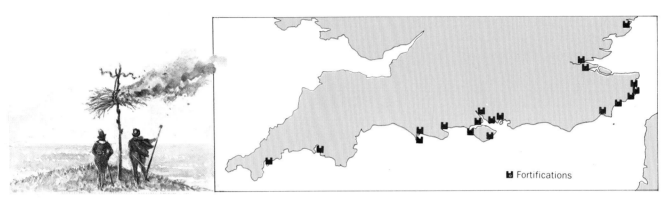

Fortifications

Parma, so he knew what to expect. Further inland the gentry were slow to raise armed bands. Being so far from the coast, they felt little danger.

Most important was the organization of the navy. John Hawkins had been hard at work designing new ships. Francis Drake created a new method of fighting. The traditional style of sea battle was for ships to come within close range of each other, grappling irons were slung from ship to ship, soldiers swung themselves onto the enemy ships and fought hand-to-hand. The ships were built with high fore and aft castles which were defended like castles on land.

Drake changed this method completely. He trained his sailors to fight by handling their ships expertly, and, by using long range guns, they could out-gun and out-manoeuvre the enemy.

John Hawkins' new English ships went into battle "line ahead", or one following the other, sailing by the enemy while firing lethal broadsides into their ships.

The Spanish had been ordered, should they engage the English ships, to bear down on them and use the old style of grappling and boarding, but the faster English vessels with their long range guns kept out of range. The battles of the Armada were the first in which the English used this method of fighting. From that time it became the normal style of encounter in sea battles.

A network of beacons was constructed on headlands and hills. It stretched like a monster cobweb across the counties of southern England. Men were posted, two by day and two by night, to light the beacons. The glow from these great bonfires could be seen across the country, signalling the arrival of the Great Armada.

The placing of warning beacons on high ground was common practice when invasion was expected in England. In 1588 almost every parish in southern England had one. Sadly many parish records have vanished, but sites of Armada Beacons are still known, the most famous being St Michael's Mount in Cornwall. Black Down, near Haslemere, was another ancient beacon restored in Elizabethan times. Near Brighton, Ditchling Beacon stands on the site of an ancient hill fort.

Both English and Spanish ships varied enormously in size. A great galleass, such as the *Girona* which sank off the Giant's Causeway, could be 50 metres long, about the length of six buses. The galleass was a combination of galley and galleon, with both oars and sails. It was a cumbersome vessel against the new English 'race' ships. The *Golden Hinde*, at 21 metres, was half the length of a Spanish galleass.

Even so the great English ships, the *Ark Royal*, the *Revenge*, the *Nonpareil*, towered above the fishing boats which put out from the south coast ports to their aid during the battles. Even before England became Protestant, her ships were given names like *Dreadnought*, *Swiftsure*, *Tiger*, *Triumph*, while Spain preferred saints' names, such as *San Martin*, *San Lorenzo* and *Rata Santa Maria Encoronada*.

The Spanish ships (above) remained heavy and more unwieldy, designed for the old style of fighting from ship to ship rather as if they were floating castles.

John Hawkins built new ships specially designed for Francis Drake's newly created type of sea battle. He also remade the old ones by cutting off the high castles. Sometimes he even had them lengthened by cutting the ships in half and inserting whole new sections. These longer, lower ships

(below) lay snug, in the water and were much easier to manage. They were called "race" ships, not because they were fast, but because the high castles had been "razed" or cut down. Being longer, they could also carry a greater number of cannon.

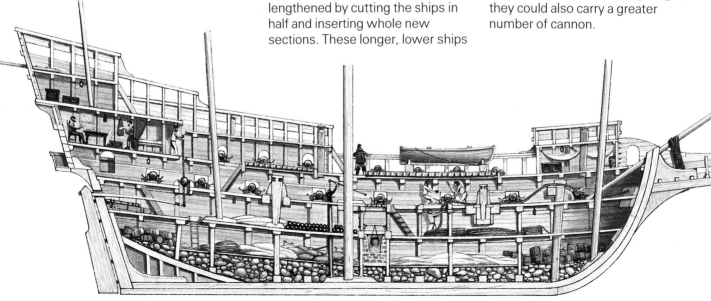

War and Weapons

By the sixteenth century gunpowder was in common use. Its immense power meant that siege warfare had become a highly technical science. The Italians were experts in the arts of war, and the Earl of Leicester employed several to design his defences. Frederico Giambelli made the defences at Tilbury strong enough to withstand the siege guns of the Spanish.

Both English and Spanish soldiers used muskets and arquebuses. Bows and arrows were still in use, and the English were famous for their expertise with the long-bow. The sixteenth century long pike, with its vicious iron point, was a lethal weapon against cavalry. Pikemen had to be fast and strong, to handle the long pike which stood about three times the height of a man. Their battle tactic was to form tight squares, with pikes held aloft, like hedgehogs. When the enemy cavalry charged, down came the pikes like a fearsome metal hedge. Halberds, the sixteenth century version of the pole-axe, were nasty weapons for hand-to-hand fighting. They were very heavy, so the halberdiers had to be extremely strong men.

Foot soldiers, such as pikemen, bowmen, halberdiers, musketeers and arquebusiers all wore some form of metal armour, and their only uniform was a bright tabard or tunic to show their squadron or army.

On board ship the gun crews worked in such hot, cramped conditions that they were usually stripped to the waist, with handkerchiefs tied round their heads to keep the sweat out of their eyes. They were unable to stand upright between the low decks. In battle the gun decks were an appalling combination of noise, heat, smoke and confusion.

The Spanish foot soldier wore a 'Morion' or helmet. His body was protected by half armour or corselet.

Two main types of cannon were used in the battles of the Armada. One was cast in a single piece of bronze and loaded from the muzzle (below). The other (right) was made on the principle of a wooden barrel with wrought-iron staves or strips and hoops welded together. It had a detachable powder chamber or breech piece.

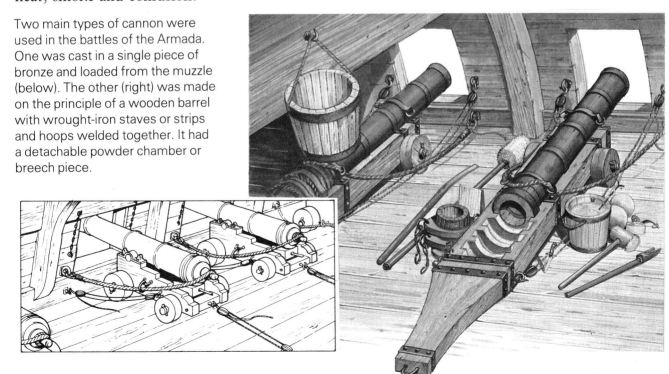

The Armada Sails

On May 11, 1588, the Great Armada set sail from Lisbon. For days the fleet had been waiting for a favourable wind. On board his flagship, the *San Martin*, the Duke of Medina ordered a great cannon to be fired as the tide turned and a light wind came up from the east. Then the deep sound of bugles across the water signalled the ships to weigh anchor and make sail. A colossal din broke out as sailors hauled in cables and hoisted sails. At last, the great adventure had begun.

Like a magnificent royal pageant the ships sailed in stately procession down river to the sea, their colourful squadron banners fluttering in the breeze, following in the wake of Medina's flagship, which flew the brilliant royal standard of

Spain. Blessed by their priests, one hundred and thirty ships carrying 30,000 men were setting out to conquer England.

However, sailing ships are at the mercy of the weather. Before the fleet reached open water, the wind changed to a strong north-west; the Great Armada was forced to anchor and shelter at the mouth of the Tagus. In the heavy swell, the Duke of Medina, like many of his sailors, became very seasick.

For over two weeks the suffering crews waited and then set sail once more. In heavy seas, through day and night, it was impossible to stay together. After three weeks, storms forced the fleet to seek shelter in Corunna. Here Medina waited for the scattered ships to assemble.

With rotting food, stinking water and many sick, it seemed foolish to go on, but Philip II insisted. A month later, with fresh supplies and ships repaired as best they could, the Great Armada set off again. This time they were lucky. The wind which took them north blew back the English fleet which had sailed out from Plymouth to stop them.

On Friday, July 29, Captain Thomas Flemyng in the *Golden Hinde* put into Plymouth to say he had sighted the Armada off the Lizard fifty miles away.

England in Wait

In the sixteenth century it was the custom for the aristocracy to command. Queen Elizabeth appointed as Lord Admiral and Commander-in-Chief of her navy her cousin, Lord Howard of Effingham. Lord Howard's father, two uncles and great grand-father had been Lords Admirals, so he had the sea in his blood. Philip II had also chosen a great noble, the Duke of Medina Sidonia, to lead the Armada.

Howard wisely appointed as his second-in-command the experienced Sir Francis Drake, who was a superb leader, with a deep knowledge of the sea, loved and admired by his sailors. He commanded the 500-ton *Revenge*, rebuilt to John Hawkins' design. Other famous sea captains in the Plymouth Squadron were Thomas Fenner, Martin Frobisher and Edward Fenton. John Hawkins was in charge of the Medway Squadron, and Lord Henry Seymour guarded the Dover Strait. The Queen's navy now consisted of 47 fighting ships. To these were added ships volunteered by gentry and noblemen at their own expense.

Peace Negotiations

Even as the Great Armada was sailing north, peace talks continued between Elizabeth and the Duke of Parma. The revolt in the Spanish Netherlands had dragged on from 1566, leaving the country in a state of chaos. By 1579, William the Silent, leader of the Protestants, was convinced that Spain would never give them freedom of religion or government.

In 1584, William the Silent was assassinated. The Catholic Duke of Parma grasped the opportunity and began to win back the northern states. In desperation, the Protestant states turned to England for help, but Elizabeth sent only a small army under the Earl of Leicester. It was agreed that two Dutch ports, Flushing and Brill, were to be governed by English commanders.

In August, 1587, Parma captured the important city of Sluys, giving him access to the sea. Leicester's army was unsuccessful and he was recalled, but English troops remained in Holland to help the Protestants. Spies kept Elizabeth informed of the movements and size of Parma's army. Philip II wanted to get the English out of Holland, and this was yet another reason for sending the Great Armada.

The Duke of Parma played for time, keeping Elizabeth's ambassadors talking, while the flyboats of the Protestant Justin of Nassau (William the Silent's son) kept up a blockade of the deep-water Dutch ports. Parma had to prepare Nieuport and Dunkirk from which to launch his ships. These ports were very shallow with shifting sandbanks. Parma expected that the Armada would destroy the English fleet and clear a passage for his barges to cross the Channel and invade England. He pretended to the English that his preparations were for a local campaign.

This confused state of affairs continued until the Armada

Country gentry were required to organize armed bands or militia. Sir Walter Raleigh, a member of Elizabeth's defence committee, was sent to raise armed bands in the West Country. Parishes also raised their own civil defence. An odd assortment of armour and arms were collected: helmets, gauntlets, corselets and girdles; swords, daggers, halberds, pikes and muskets. We have no idea of the condition of these arms, but much of it was probably old and rusty, and country folk had only farm tools as weapons.

Why did the Duke of Parma, the greatest military leader in Europe, fail to embark his troops? Parma reported that his barges, laden with troops, could only reach England in fine weather, and if escorted by the Armada. He told the King that the big Spanish ships would not find deep anchorage near Dunkirk and that enemy flyboats would prevent him from coming out. Philip never reported this to Medina, who on approaching Dunkirk was appalled to find no safe anchorage.

entered the English Channel and had its first encounter with Elizabeth's navy.

Elizabeth was also playing for time, assembling her fleet and mobilizing her troops. The Spanish War Council had distributed a list of all items of the Armada, including torture instruments: a piece of propaganda intended to terrify the enemy. The Spaniards did not disclose their plan of action and Elizabeth's secret agents had no idea where the Armada would land. The English thought it would be the mouth of the Thames, where Leicester was frantically building defences at Tilbury and near Gravesend. In fact, the Spanish planned to land near Margate, an area poorly defended by the English. Altogether, the English land defences were haphazard and unfinished. It was, therefore, of the utmost importance that the navy was powerful enough to prevent the Spaniards from landing.

Elizabeth was cautious. She did not want England to fire the first shot. Drake thought differently. He was convinced the way to beat the Spanish was to attack them in their own ports. When he heard the Armada was halted by storms at Corunna, he persuaded the Queen to let him take a fleet to attack them. But his ships were beaten back by bad weather.

On July 31, near the Eddystone, the Duke of Medina, like a knight of old, hoisted the standard of Spain on the main topmast of his flagship, the *San Martin*. It was the signal to begin the battle. Lord Howard sent the *Disdain* to accept the challenge. Then Howard, in his flagship, the *Ark Royal*, led out his squadron in line ahead. The war between England and Spain had begun.

4: Engagement

Encounter

When Sir Francis Drake heard that the Great Armada had been sighted off the Lizard, he was playing bowls on Plymouth Hoe. He made the now legendary comment: "There is plenty of time to finish the game, and beat the Spaniards." In fact Drake had time to spare. It was low tide, and impossible to take the fleet out of harbour for another eight hours.

When they did set sail with 54 ships, it was raining so hard the fleets could scarcely see each other. In sailing ships the most important tactic in battle is to get to the windward of the enemy. Then a captain can sail his ship into the attack, while his enemy has the wind blowing against him. To get to windward or "win the weather gauge" is vital. The Spaniards admired the ability of the new English ships to win the weather gauge. The English were deeply impressed by the discipline of the Spaniards and how they kept close formation. In this first encounter a few shots were fired, but little damage was done.

So the Armada sailed on, followed by the English. Two great Spanish ships were put out of action by accident. The *Rosario* collided with others and was disabled. At dawn on Sunday, August 1, she was captured by Drake and towed into Torbay. Her commander Don Pedro de Valdes, was taken prisoner. Recalde's *San Salvador* blew up with tremendous loss of life. She was abandoned and the English towed her into Weymouth. Aboard

The course of the Armada from the Lizard to Gravelines is a distance of about 279 miles. The Armada was spread out in a great arc, like a huge bird with a seven-mile wingspan. The Duke of Medina led in his flagship, the *San Martin*, with a vanguard of principal battleships. In the centre were clustered the slow-moving urcas or transports, closely guarded in the rear by the experienced Recalde with his Biscayan Squadron. On the wings were some of the most powerful galleons.

After the first encounter off the Eddystone, the Spanish changed their battle order and put some of their best warships in the rear to beat off the harrying English.

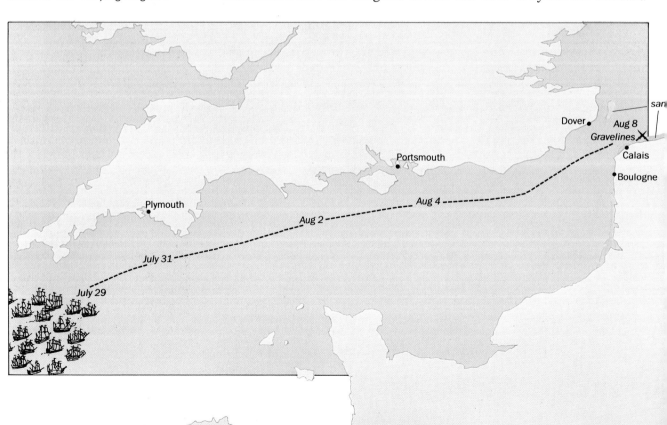

her they found 2000 cannon balls and 140 barrels of gunpowder, which were quickly taken by the *Golden Hinde* to the main fleet.

On August 2, off Portland Bill the second battle took place. This time the Spanish had the advantage of the weather gauge. At long range little damage was done. The English reported the "waste of a terrible value of shot". The fragile rigging and castles of the Spanish ships were easily penetrated, but not their solid hulls. The Spanish could not get close enough to grapple and board the English vessels.

On August 4, as the Isle of Wight came into view, the Duke of Medina, with the English hard on his heels, had many things on his mind. Ammunition was running low. He had sent messages to Parma, with no response. Now his letters, sent by pinnace, became more urgent, asking for shot.

The English were determined to prevent the Spanish entering the Solent. In calm weather, Howard ordered the *Ark Royal* to be towed into battle by rowboats, followed by the *Golden Lion*. Three Spanish galleasses detached themselves from the fleet to do battle. For hours the great ships pounded each other, watched by their fleets. Then the wind rose to the Spaniards' advantage, but again the nimble English got away. With a south-west wind the Great Armada continued towards the Straits of Dover, in the hope of meeting Parma at Dunkirk. As he sailed, Medina was given the appalling news that there was no anchorage deep enough for the fleet on the Flemish shore.

From the cliffs and shore people watched in amazement at the grand spectacle as the Armada, like a stately pageant of gilded ships, their banners flying, sailed up the Channel. Behind them came the English, equally magnificent, bristling with cannon, their upper decks gleaming with gold carvings and brilliantly coloured coats of arms. What were the watchers' feelings? Fear, or pride that the Queen's splendid navy kept the Spanish out to sea? Off the Isle of Wight the boom of heavy guns could be heard as Lord Howard led his ships into the attack to prevent the Spaniards from entering the Solent. Then the Spanish continued on their way; the English ships in hot pursuit.

Fire at Sea

Little damage could be done to the Great Armada on the move. With the great fleet forced to anchor off Calais it was a different matter. Now was the time to send in fireships. The Spanish knew that the Italian engineer, Giambelli, had made fireships laden with explosives for the English. These "Hellburners" were the most fearful weapons for a fleet at anchor.

The Spanish began to prepare. Pinnaces stood guard with long grapnels to tow the fireships away from the main fleet. Medina ordered the ships to be ready to weigh anchor for a quick getaway. As it was a lengthy business hauling up heavy sea anchors, the tactic was to attach them to buoys. If the fireships came, then the ships cut their cables and escaped, leaving the heavy anchors attached to the buoys. When the danger was over the ships could return to pick up the anchors.

Lord Howard's squadrons were joined by the Dover Squadron, led by Lord Henry Seymour. Now the Queen's navy almost equalled the Armada in number. The English recognized their advantage. They filled eight old ships with inflammable material and waited for the wind and tide.

After midnight, the waiting Spaniards saw the glow from the fireships approaching on the tide. As they came closer, their guns heated and exploded, making a terrifying sight. The Spanish hastily cut their cables. In the pitch darkness they collided with each other in their effort to escape. The huge galleass, the *San Lorenzo*, was badly damaged, but no ship was set on fire.

In "An Engagement between the English and Spanish Fleets", (right) the great galleass flies the red flag of Spain with a gold cross, while the English fly the white flag of St George with its red cross. Striped flags indicate individual squadrons.

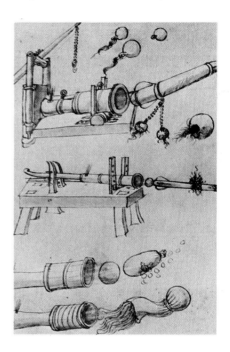

Cannon were loaded from the muzzle end. The gunpowder, wrapped in cloth, was pushed down the barrel, followed by wadding, rammed into place to hold the powder and keep it dry. At the word of command, the gunner lit his linstock, put it to the touch-hole in the barrel and the gun fired.

This contemporary map tells three stories. The English squadrons (1) sail out from Plymouth. The Armada (2) challenges the English and battle takes place south of the Eddystone rock. The English fleet (3) chases the Armada south of Start Point. The battle formations are imaginary and would have been far less orderly.

The Battle of Gravelines

At daylight on August 8, Medina realized many of his ships were in danger of running on the shoals of the Flemish coast, an easy target for the pursuing English. With four great ships he decided to stand and fight, desperately determined to hold off the English while the rest of the Armada collected and made ready for the coming assault.

Drake, in the *Revenge*, led the attack. One by one his squadron followed, opening fire at a hundred yards range. Frobisher's squadron followed Drake's. The Spaniards were outnumbered by about ten to one. The English had the wind behind them, and at close range their culverins made huge holes in the Spanish hulls. Spanish sails, rigging and castles were shattered. The pumps of the *San Martin* worked desperately to keep her afloat.

In the noise, smoke and confusion it was impossible to see what was happening. Other ships gathered, but the main battle was between Drake's ships and the big galleons of the Portuguese and Seville squadrons. Three great Spanish ships sank that day, a dozen more were badly damaged. 600 Spaniards were killed and at least 800 wounded. The decks ran with their blood.

Towards evening after nine gruelling hours, heavy rain and wind brought the battle to an end. But worse was to come. Amid the wreckage and blood and the screams of wounded men, the winds blew the helpless Spanish ships towards the treacherous sandbanks. When dawn came the English moved in and the exhausted Spaniards prepared themselves for death. But the English were almost out of ammunition. No attack came.

Slowly the Spaniards sounded their way through the shallow waters. At any moment they might feel the terrible lurch of a ship grounded on the sands. Then in the afternoon the wind changed and blew them away from the deadly sandbanks. The Duke of Medina wrote: "We were saved by the wind, by God's mercy, it shifted to the south-west."

The English ships received little damage. Scarcely one hundred Englishmen had died since the first encounter.

Why did the great Spanish guns do so little damage? One answer may be that their cannon balls were badly cast and splintered when fired. Their gunpowder was finer ground than the English, and perhaps was unsuited to the heavy cannon. Their guns may even have exploded on their gundecks. The merchant ships were not built to take either the weight or the recoil of heavy cannon. Continual pounding from their own guns put an immense strain on the ships' timbers. Their carpenters had the never-ending task of caulking the leaks. Sometimes the guns were not properly lashed to the gundecks. When fired, the recoil sent the guns bounding across the decks, severely damaging both ships and men.

Pursuit and Confusion

After the encounter at Gravelines, Lord Howard sent frantic messages ashore for more ammunition. He did not know that the Spanish were equally short of powder and had no great shot left. Two big crippled Portuguese galleons, the *San Felipe* and the *San Mateo*, went aground on the Dutch coast, where the flyboats of Justin of Nassau, waiting like vultures, swept down and plundered them.

The Great Armada ran north before the wind which had blown it off the Flemish sandbanks. The English followed, leaving Lord Henry Seymour's squadron behind to guard the Straits of Dover. They feared the Duke of Parma would appear with his army, but he never came.

On board the *San Martin*, Medina and his advisers decided that, should the wind change, they would return to make one more attempt to link up with Parma, or attack and seize an English port. But the English held on grimly, determined to prevent the Spanish from landing on English soil. Howard followed all the way to the Firth of Forth where he gave the order to give up the chase.

Queen Elizabeth did not realize how courageously her navy had fought and grumbled that no treasure had been captured. Only

This map shows the course of the Armada as it sailed northwards pursued by the English ships. Many ships never reached home. They battled with terrible weather and were sunk and wrecked around the inhospitable shores of Ireland.

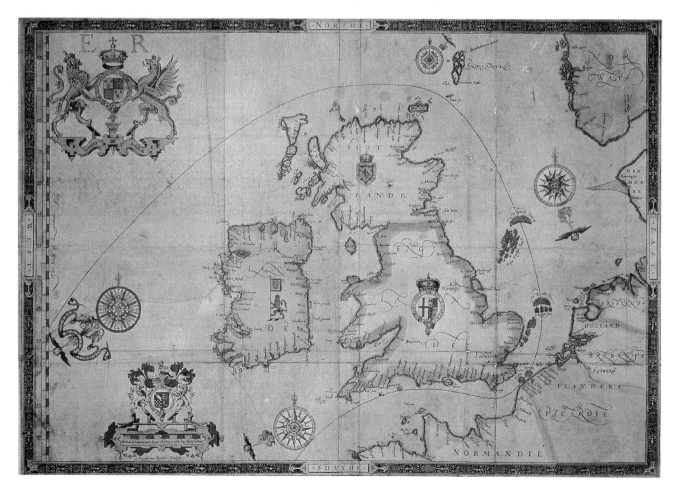

gradually did it become clear to the English that they had won a great victory and the Spanish would not return.

The End of the Armada

When the English fleet turned back, Medina and his captains held a council of war. Now their task was to get the Armada safely back to Spain. Medina wrote to the King that "the Armada was so crippled and scattered, it seemed my first duty to Your Majesty to save it, even at the risk of a very long voyage in high latitudes." The Armada was in no condition to turn back and fight its way through the Channel. Besides the wind was still taking it north. They decided to sail around Scotland and southward in the Atlantic, keeping well away from Ireland, back to Spain.

The English, having given up the chase, sent two pinnaces to shadow the Armada as far as the Orkneys. Then they headed south. The veteran Captain Thomas Fenner of the *Non Pareil* wrote predicting the fate of the Armada. As he wrote another terrible storm arose.

Spanish accounts of this storm describe the scattering of the fleet. But the Armada held on course. On August 19, in a moderate wind, they sailed safely through the Fair Isle channel between Shetland and the Orkneys, where Scottish fishermen sold them fish. Food was running out. Only a little slimy green water was left in the unseasoned wooden casks. Most of the ships biscuit, salt beef and salt fish had gone bad. Medina had to ration the food, giving each man a daily allowance of eight ounces of biscuit, and a pint of half wine half water. Horses and mules were thrown overboard.

Of the 130 ships which had set sail from Lisbon, eight great ships had been sunk. Many pinnaces and small craft had been swept away. Half the remaining ships needed drastic repairs.

Every Spanish ship was equipped with wood for making rudders, spars for masts, oxhides and lead to patch holes, tar and oakum to caulk seams. As the Armada sailed towards Scotland, repairs were carried out. The decks of the battered ships became busy workshops as the crews tried to make them seaworthy.

Marco Aramburu, commander of
San Juan Bautista, was helpless in
the Atlantic storms. On September
15, he sighted two ships off the
County Kerry coast: Recalde's *San
Juan* and a frigate. The three ships
managed to anchor in the calm
waters of Blasket Sound. On the
mainland English troops were lying
in wait. After a week a storm arose
and the ships began to drag their
anchors. Recalde's and Aramburu's
ships collided. As the sailors
worked to free them the huge
Santa Maria de la Rosa entered the
Sound. She fired a gun to say she
was in distress, and managed to
lower one anchor. For two hours
the ships struggled to maintain the
anchorage. Then the *Santa Maria*
dragged her cable across
Aramburu's and, to the onlookers'
horror, sank with all hands. The
Girona later ran onto the rocks near
the Giant's Causeway (right).

5: The Price of War

An Awful Return

Off the Orkneys, Medina sent a message to the King to say that the Armada was still together, and capable of getting back to Spain, although, besides the wounded, there were 3000 sick on board. But soon the moderate weather changed and in the terrible seas off Cape Wrath the Armada began to break up.

In gale force winds the fleet was swept backwards and forwards around the north of Scotland, facing a fiercer enemy than the English: the cruel sea. The groaning, leaking ships were kept afloat by tired, hungry men working non-stop at the pumps. Scurvy, dysentery and fever were rife. Many ships sought land looking for food and water. Because they had abandoned their sea anchors at Calais and had only small anchors, they were often driven onto the rocks. As the weather worsened ships were swept away from the main body of the fleet. Many sank with all hands.

Four great ships were blown back towards Shetland. The *Castello Negro* was never seen again. On September 1, the *Barca de Amburg* fired a gun to signal she was sinking. The *Gran Grifon* took off her crew, many of them wounded and dying, but was herself wrecked off Fair Isle a month later. All her 300 crew were saved, though many died afterwards of hunger and fever. On September 17, the *Trinidad Valencera* struck a reef off north-east Ireland. Of the 450 men aboard, some of whom had been rescued from other ships, only 32 reached France. The rest had been slaughtered, or died of exposure or fever.

About September 18 one of the worst storms hit the Atlantic. The *Rata Santa Maria Encoronada* and the *Duquesa Santa Ana* took refuge in Blacksod Bay, County Mayo. The *Rata* was shaken by battles and the buffetings of the storms, but worst of all, she too had lost her sea anchors. In the rising wind and tide she dragged her remaining anchor and grounded on the shelving beach. Her commander, the glamorous Don Alonso de Leyva, transferred his men to the *Santa Ana*. This was a tremendous feat, as the *Santa Ana* was anchored in another part of the bay and de Leyva had to march his men miles across a bleak headland through bogs and across rivers. The heavily laden ship set sail for Scotland, but was driven on the rocks at Loughros More in County Donegal. With great courage de Leyva, who had broken his leg, got his crew ashore. They had news that three Spanish ships were sheltering in the harbour of Killybegs. So again they set out across the mountains. At Killybegs they discovered that two of the ships were wrecked. 1300 men crammed onto the *Girona* and again set sail for Scotland. In the night the wind changed to a northern gale. The *Girona* hit a reef near the Giant's Causeway. Less than ten men survived; everyone else was drowned, including de Leyva who had led his men so gallantly.

In 1967 Robert Stenuit dived at the spot where local people said the *Girona* lay. He found pieces of jewellery: gold rings, bracelets, chains, crucifixes, and a tiny pendant, a beautiful salamander, the symbol of endurance. This treasure is now in the Ulster Museum, Belfast, a moving reminder of the men who met their end in such appalling circumstances.

A Famous Escape

Over a year after the defeat of the Armada a gentleman in Spain received a letter from a friend in Antwerp. The friend was Don Francisco de Cuellar, who was thought to have died in a wreck off the coast of Ireland.

When Cuellar's ship with two others had been swept into Sligo Bay, they dared not risk a landing. Ireland was wild and unruly, and English soldiers patrolled the coasts, fearing a Spanish invasion. A severe storm drove the three ships onto the beach, and over 1000 men drowned. Cuellar grabbed a hatch cover and was swept onto the shore, smashing his leg on a timber.

Half-naked, shivering and covered in blood, he escaped the plundering Irish and made for the woods. A beautiful girl fed him, although she took his Order of the Holy Trinity from his neck. He was helped by a priest in disguise, with whom he conversed in Latin. Then, gathering more fugitive Spaniards, he found safety in Rossclogher Castle, home of Dartry, Chief of the MacClancy clan.

The English Lord Deputy, Sir William Fitzwilliam, had raised an army of 1700 men to exterminate the Spaniards and punish their Irish helpers. The MacClancys could not hold out against such a force, so they fled to the mountains. Cuellar and his twelve companions remained to defend the castle, armed with four boatloads of stones, six muskets and six crossbows. The castle, set in a bog and partly surrounded by water, was difficult to attack. After seventeen days, a bitter snowstorm sent the English marching back to Dublin. The MacClancys returned and Dartry

A bucket from the wreck of the 1,100 ton Sicilian merchant ship *Trinidad Valencera*, which ran aground in Kinnagoe Bay, County Donegal in September, 1588.

offered his sister in marriage to Cuellar, begging the Spaniards to stay. But Cuellar was intent on getting home to Spain.

With four companions he left the Castle secretly before dawn. He ran into some English soldiers, but once more he was rescued by women who hid him. Eventually he met a bishop who smuggled him, with other Spanish fugitives, to Scotland. A Scottish merchant took him to Flanders where the Duke of Parma was paying five ducats for each returned Spaniard. His luck held to the end. Though marauding Dutch flyboats sank his ship, he scrambled ashore at Dunkirk: one of three who survived out of 270 Spaniards who went down with his ship.

The English Aftermath

Why did the English ships stop following the Armada near the Firth of Forth? Despite the damage to the Armada at the Battle of Gravelines, only a few Spanish ships were put out of action, both fleets had run out of ammunition and the English badly needed to replenish their food and water.

On August 11, Howard, Drake and other captains wrote to the Privy Council saying that, because food and ammunition were "in extreme scarcity", they would pursue the Armada only until it was clear of the English coast. On August 22, Howard wrote saying "the fleet is grievously infected, and men die daily." Dysentery, typhus and, some thought, plague swept the fleet.

The English ships staggered back into Harwich, Margate, Chatham and Dover. Sir John Hawkins had hoped to organize a general discharge, but the sick were let go little by little: some with no more than a ticket to buy food for the journey home; some with only part of the money due to them. Howard beseeched the government: "before God, I would rather have never a penny in the world, than that they should lack," and dipped into his own pocket to pay off many poor sailors.

Gradually the English realized that the Great Armada would not return. The jubilant Queen Elizabeth turned it into a personal triumph. In December 1588, she rode, like a conquering Caesar, to give thanks at St Paul's Cathedral. Among the prayers of thanksgiving, she listened to the singing of her own composition:

"He made the winds and waters rise,
To scatter all mine Enemies."

The poor starving or wounded seamen and soldiers who had defeated the Armada dragged themselves home as best they could. Those who lay dying in the streets of Chatham and the east coast towns had no one to care for them. Their appalling condition prompted the compassion of Hawkins, who with Howard and Drake, began to collect sixpence a month for "poor sailors maimed in the navy."

The Aftermath

When Philip was told the dreadful news of his splendid ships, he said, "I sent them to fight against men, not storms." Regardless of cost, he set about building better ships and making more powerful arms to overcome the English.

Elizabeth's treasury was almost empty, but, with money collected from the City of London and her courtiers, she sent a fleet of 126 ships, commanded by Drake, to attack the remains of the Armada in Santander. But Drake and his captains wanted booty as well as naval victory and sailed to Corunna, hoping to attack Lisbon. Sickness broke out among the crews, and bad weather dispersed the ships. The dispirited fleet straggled back to Plymouth. The Queen was furious and Drake was in disgrace for several years.

Five years later Philip II sent 100 ships to invade England, but more than half of them were destroyed by a fierce gale in the Bay of Biscay. The following year another Spanish fleet almost reached the Lizard, but once again the "winds of God" blew them back to Spain.

The "Peacemakers" confer at Somerset House in London in 1604. On the left of the window sits the Constable of Castile, leader of the Spanish Flemish delegation. On the right are the English. Second from the right is Howard of Effingham, right front is Robert Cecil, first Earl of Salisbury.

The 'Armada Portrait' of Elizabeth I was painted to celebrate England's victory. Magnificently dressed, loaded with jewels, with a ruff of the most delicate lace, the Queen sits with her right hand on the globe. Behind her scenes represent victory over the Armada. She was 56 at the time, yet appears eternally young, a symbol of her power to lead her people.

In 1595, Drake, now back in favour with the Queen, set out on an expedition with Hawkins to capture treasure in the Caribbean. They were old men now by sixteenth century standards: Drake was 55, Hawkins, over 60. Near Porto Rico Hawkins fell ill and died. The Spanish were waiting with a powerful force and beat off the raiders. Drake, sad and ill with dysentery, died and was buried at sea off Puerto Bello.

In June, 1596, a magnificent fleet of 150 ships led by Howard of Effingham, Sir Walter Raleigh and the young Earl of Essex plundered Cadiz and set fire to it. In the inner harbour the Spanish fired their own ships to prevent the English from capturing treasure worth 12,000,000 ducats. The Queen had helped fit out the fleet, and was furious with Essex for bringing back only £13,000 of booty.

Philip II of Spain died in 1598 and his son became Philip III. Still the war with England dragged on. In 1601 Spain sent her last Armada against England. A force of 500 Spanish soldiers landed at Kinsale in Ireland to help the native Irish rebellion. For three months the combined forces held out, until the more powerful English army defeated them. Sir George Carew sent the captured Spaniards home without asking for ransom. The Spanish general sent him a crate of wine and oranges to thank him for his generosity.

Peace at Last
During these disruptive years of war the English cloth trade declined. There was a boom in shipbuilding and England's forests were stripped of timber.

When Elizabeth died in 1603, James VI of Scotland became James I of England, the first Stuart monarch. He was determined to end the long war between England and Spain and in 1604 peace talks began at Somerset House in London. He started to plan a marriage for his son with the daughter of the Spanish king, just as Henry VII, the first Tudor monarch, had done over a century before. But this marriage never took place.

National Trust Properties connected with the Armada Story

Buckland Abbey, in Devon, was built as a monastery in the 13th century. It was owned later by Sir Richard Grenville of the *Revenge*, who sold it to Sir Francis Drake in 1581, on his return from sailing round the world. Here, Drake planned his voyage to Cadiz to "singe the King of Spain's beard".

All around the south-west defences were prepared to repel a Spanish invasion. Local landowners were put in charge of protecting stretches of coast. At *St Michael's Mount*, in Cornwall, the Constable, Sir Francis Godolphin, used a beacon on top of the church tower to signal the approach of the Spanish fleet. Seven years later, when the Spanish returned to launch fresh attacks on Newlyn, he had to raise the militia to force them to take to their ships. The Carews of *Antony House* and the Edgcumbes of *Cotehele* also helped to organize Cornwall's defences in 1588.

Along the coast, *Compton Castle*, in Devon, was the home of John and Humphrey Gilbert and their half-brother, Walter Raleigh. John was put in charge of the defence of the area and the port of Dartmouth. The Gilbert brothers supplied several vessels for the English fleet. During the fighting, the galleon *Rosario* was captured and brought into Torbay by Raleigh's *Roebuck*. Further east still, defences were renewed on *Brownsea Island* in Poole Harbour, Dorset, now a nature reserve.

There are Armada beacon sites at *Black Down*, West Sussex; *Ditchling*, East Sussex; *Dunkery* on Exmoor, Somerset; *St Michael's Mount*, Cornwall.

Off the Co. Antrim coast, in Northern Ireland, close to the

Giant's Causeway, the galleass *Girona* foundered on October 28 1588 as she made her painful way homewards with the remnant of the Spanish fleet. 1295 lives were lost. In 1968 many treasures were salvaged, which can now be seen in the Ulster Museum, Belfast.

Hardwick Hall, in Derbyshire, was built by Bess of Hardwick, Countess of Shrewsbury, who guarded Mary Queen of Scots for Elizabeth I through much of her long imprisonment. In fact, there are two Halls which stand side by side. Both were built by Bess. The second, a much larger mansion, was built with the money she inherited from her husband in 1590. Embroidery made by Bess and Mary can be seen at Hardwick.

Oxburgh Hall, in Norfolk, contains wall hangings with panels worked by Mary Queen of Scots and Bess of Hardwick.

In the long gallery at *Montacute*, Somerset, hang many Tudor and Elizabethan portraits from the National Portrait Gallery. Among them are Elizabeth I, Mary Tudor, Mary Queen of Scots, Francis Drake and many others involved in the story of the Armada.

Elizabeth's Catholic subjects were faced with a mixture of allegiances: heart to Elizabeth but soul to the Pope, and hence Philip II. The Throckmortons of *Coughton Court*, Warwickshire, were a leading Catholic family. Their home contains many reminders of their loyalty to the Catholic Faith when its practice was against the law.